LUNGLESS
Salamanders

by Emily Hudd

Content Consultant

Gian L. Rocco
Project Manager/Wildlife Biologist
Western EcoSystems Technology

CAPSTONE PRESS
a capstone imprint

Bright Idea Books are published by Capstone Press
1710 Roe Crest Drive, North Mankato, Minnesota 56003
www.mycapstone.com

Library of Congress Cataloging-in-Publication Data
Names: Hudd, Emily, author.
Title: Lungless salamanders / by Emily Hudd.
Description: North Mankato, Minnesota : Capstone Press, [2020] | Series:
   Unique animal adaptations | Audience: Grade 4 to 6. | Includes
   bibliographical references and index.
Identifiers: LCCN 2018061084 (print) | LCCN 2019000097 (ebook) | ISBN
   9781543571745 (ebook) | ISBN 9781543571547 (hardcover) | ISBN 9781543575088 (paperback)
Subjects: LCSH: Lungless salamanders--Juvenile literature. | Lungless
   salamanders--Adaptation--Juvenile literature.
Classification: LCC QL668.C274 (ebook) | LCC QL668.C274 H83 2020 (print) |
   DDC 597.8/59--dc23
LC record available at https://lccn.loc.gov/2018061084

All internet sites appearing in back matter were available and accurate when this book was sent to press.

Editorial Credits
Editor: Marie Pearson
Designer: Becky Daum
Production Specialist: Colleen McLaren

Photo Credits
Newscom: Rauschenbach, F./picture alliance/Arco Images G, 14; Shutterstock Images: Federico. Crovetto, 6–7, 17, 29, Frank Reiser, 21, Jason Patrick Ross, 22–23, Jay Ondreicka, cover, 5, 9, 12–13, 18–19, 25, 28, 30–31, Nashepard, 10, Oliver Fahle, 27

Design Elements: Red Line Editorial

Printed in the United States of America.
PA70

TABLE OF CONTENTS

CHAPTER 1

LUNGLESS Salamanders

See that long, glossy creature under the rock? It is a lungless salamander! Lungless salamanders are amphibians. Amphibians can breathe through their skin.

Lungless salamanders have smooth skin. They can be red or orange. They can be brown or gray. Black spots may cover their skin.

Lungless salamanders come in many colors.

Most lungless salamanders are small. Their heads and bodies are 1.5 to 5 inches (4 to 12 centimeters) long. Each salamander has four legs and a tail. The tail is longer than the body. Sometimes it is twice as long as the body.

SHORT LEGS

Lungless salamanders' legs are very short. Their bellies drag on the ground when they walk!

There are more than 250 **species** of lungless salamanders. Most live in North and South America. Many live in forests. They crawl on the ground. They live in **habitats** with water.

A forest has shade and water for lungless salamanders.

CHAPTER 2

ADAPTATIONS

Lungless salamanders have **adapted** to their environment. Most animals need oxygen to live. Oxygen is a gas. It gives the body energy. Many animals breathe oxygen with their lungs. But lungless salamanders do not have lungs. They breathe through their skin. Lungs fill with air. This would make their bodies float in water. So they have adapted to breathe without lungs.

These animals dive into the water to catch food. They hide on the bottom of streams or under rocks to escape predators.

Lungless salamanders use their skin to breathe.

Lungless salamanders need wet skin to breathe. The skin **absorbs** oxygen from the air and water. Too much wind or sunshine can dry the skin. Then the animals can't breathe.

Lungless salamanders use their mouths to help them breathe.

The salamanders also breathe through a **lining** in the mouth. The lining flutters to move the air. It pulls in oxygen from the air.

CAVE SPECIES

Some species of salamanders live in caves. Their bodies change as they grow. They adapt to the dark habitat. Their skin loses color. Their eyes disappear. Their eyelids close up.

SPECIAL BODIES

Lungless salamanders' bodies cannot create heat. They cannot sweat to cool off. They use the environment. They lie in the sun to warm up. They find shade under rocks or plants to stay cool.

Lungless salamanders might hide under damp moss to keep cool.

Some lungless salamanders eat insects.

Salamanders do not have ears. They can't hear sounds. Some have sensitive bodies. They can feel **vibrations**.

Some salamanders have strong tongues. They flick them when food gets close. Their tongues catch small worms and insects.

CHAPTER 3

LIFE Cycle

Female lungless salamanders lay eggs. One female can lay 1 to 450 eggs. Some lay eggs on land or underwater. They place the eggs in **moss** or under rocks. Then they guard the eggs.

PROTECTING EGGS

Females have different ways of protecting their eggs. Some put their bodies around the eggs. Some wrap leaves around them. The eggs stay hidden.

Females protect their eggs until they hatch.

17

Gills grow from a larva's neck.

After a few weeks, the young salamanders hatch. Some hatch with their adult form. But most hatch as **larvae**. They have four legs and a tail. They look like tiny adults. But they have **gills**. They live in water.

Larvae eat tiny insects and plants that float in the water. They don't eat the same food as the adults. This helps them survive.

Larvae grow and change. Their bodies get bigger. Their gills disappear. Some become adults in just three months. Others aren't adults until they are more than four years old. Many leave the water. They live on land.

Lungless salamander larvae sometimes eat mosquito larvae (pictured).

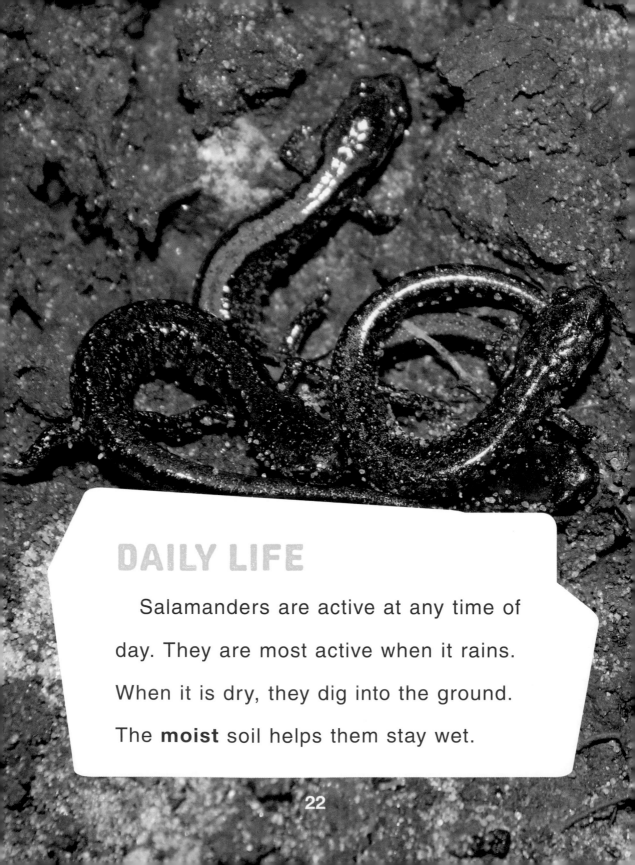

DAILY LIFE

Salamanders are active at any time of day. They are most active when it rains. When it is dry, they dig into the ground. The **moist** soil helps them stay wet.

Multiple lungless salamanders live in the same area.

Lungless salamanders live in groups. Most live for about 10 years. Adults live in the same area their whole lives.

STAYING
Safe

Big animals eat lungless salamanders. Salamanders have to be careful. They do not have tough skin. Hiding is their best **defense**. They hide under things or in small spaces.

Hiding is one way lungless salamanders stay safe.

Clean environments help lungless salamanders survive. Trees shade the ground. Plants keep the soil moist and healthy. Most importantly, salamanders need water. People help them survive by taking care of the environment.

Scientists study lungless salamanders to learn how to help them survive.

GLOSSARY

absorb
to take in

adapt
to have differences that help
a species fit into a new or
different environment

defense
how an animal protects itself

female
an animal of the sex that can
lay eggs or have babies

gill
an organ that helps an animal
breathe in water

habitat
the place where an
animal lives

larva
a baby salamander that
hatches from an egg and has
a different body than adults;
the plural is larvae

lining
a thin layer of skin

moist
a little wet and not dry

moss
a type of plant that is soft
and wet

species
a specific type of animal

vibration
a small movement carried
through the ground or air

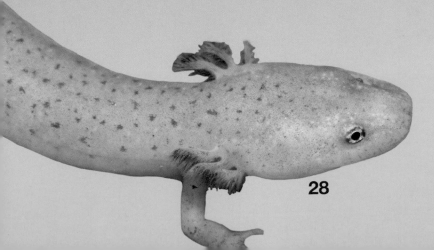

TRIVIA

1. Lungless salamanders adapted to water habitats by learning to breathe without lungs.

2. Female lungless salamanders can lay up to 450 eggs.

3. Lungless salamanders are more active when it rains.

4. Lungless salamanders belong to the scientific family Plethodontidae.

ACTIVITY

STAYING MOIST

Imagine you needed moist skin like a lungless salamander. Write a paragraph about how you would keep from drying out. What conditions might dry out your skin? Where could you go if you needed to make your skin moist? What places would you have to avoid or risk drying out?

31

FURTHER RESOURCES

Amazed by salamanders? Learn more here:

Gish, Melissa. *Salamanders.* Living Wild. Mankato, Minn.: Creative Education, 2018.

Guillain, Charlotte. *Life Story of a Salamander.* Animal Life Stories. Chicago, Ill: Heinemann Library, 2015.

San Diego Zoo: Salamander and Newt
https://animals.sandiegozoo.org/animals/salamander-and-newt

Ready to learn about other amphibians? Check out these resources:

Mattison, Chris. *Reptiles and Amphibians.* New York: DK Publishing, 2017.

National Geographic Kids: Amphibians
https://kids.nationalgeographic.com/animals/hubs/amphibians/

San Diego Zoo: Amphibians
https://animals.sandiegozoo.org/animals/amphibians

INDEX

NIGHT WITCHES AT WAR

THE SOVIET WOMEN PILOTS OF WORLD WAR II

by Bruce Berglund
illustrated by Trevor Goring

Consultant:
Tim Solie
Adjunct Professor of History
Minnesota State University, Mankato
Mankato, Minnesota

CAPSTONE PRESS
a capstone imprint

Graphic Library is published by Capstone Press,
1710 Roe Crest Drive, North Mankato, Minnesota 56003
www.capstonepub.com

Library of Congress Cataloging-in-Publication data
Names: Berglund, Bruce R., author. | Goring, Trevor, 1952– illustrator.
Title: Night Witches at war : the Soviet women pilots of World War II / by Bruce Berglund ;
    illustrated by Trevor Goring.
Description: North Mankato : Capstone Press, [2020] | Series: Graphic library amazing
    World War II stories | Audience: Ages: 8–14. | Audience: Grades: 4–6. | Includes
    bibliographical references and index.
Identifiers: LCCN 2019005962 (print) | LCCN 2019014190 (ebook) | ISBN 9781543573190
    (eBook PDF) | ISBN 9781543573152 (library binding) | ISBN 9781543575507 (paperback)
Subjects: LCSH: Soviet Union. Raboche-Krestianskaia Krasnaia Armiia. Voenno-Vozdushnye
    Sily—History—Juvenile literature. | World War, 1939–1945—Aerial operations, Soviet—
    Juvenile literature. | Women air pilots—Soviet Union—History—Juvenile literature. |
    Bomber pilots—Soviet Union—History—Juvenile literature. | Night flying—Soviet Union—
    History—Juvenile literature. | World War, 1939–1945—Women—Soviet Union—Juvenile
    literature.
Classification: LCC D792.S65 (ebook) | LCC D792.S65 B485 2020 (print) |
    DDC 940.54/4947—dc23
LC record available at https://lccn.loc.gov/2019005962

Summary: In graphic novel format, tells the amazing story of the Soviet Night Witches and their
courage while flying nighttime bombing missions on the front lines during World War II.

EDITOR
Aaron J. Sautter

ART DIRECTOR
Nathan Gassman

DESIGNER
Ted Williams

PRODUCTION SPECIALIST
Katy LaVigne

Design Elements by Shutterstock/Guenter Albers

All internet sites appearing in back matter were available and accurate when this book was sent
to press.

Direct quotations appear in **bold italicized text** on the following pages:
Pages 7, 9: from *Wings, Women, and War: Soviet Airwomen in World War II Combat*, by
    Reina Pennington, Lawrence, KS: University Press of Kansas, 2002.
Page 29, panel 2: from "Women Veterans of Aviation in the Soviet Union," by Reina Pennington
    in *A Soldier and a Woman: Sexual Integration in the Military*, edited by Gerard J. DeGroot
    and C.M. Peniston-Bird. New York: Pearson Education, 2000.
Page 29, panel 3: from "Nadezhda Popova, WWII 'Night Witch,' Dies at 91," by Douglas Martin,
    The New York Times, July 14, 2013. https://www.nytimes.com/2013/07/15/world/europe/
    nadezhda-popova-ww-ii-night-witch-dies-at-91.html

Printed and bound in China. 5174

TABLE OF CONTENTS

UNDER ATTACK

Nearly two years after World War II (1939–1945) began, Nazi Germany launched the largest military invasion the world had ever seen on June 22, 1941.

More than 3 million soldiers, 3,000 tanks, 7,000 artillery, and 3,000 airplanes crossed the border into the Soviet Union.

Soviet forces were caught by surprise. Thousands of planes were destroyed before they could take off.

The Nazis bombed many Soviet cities and villages. Millions of people died—more than in any other country during World War II.

People across the Soviet Union volunteered to defend their homeland.

Many women and teenage girls joined the army. Others joined their neighbors and used whatever weapons they could find.

Some women became pilots and fought the Nazis from the skies.

German forces soon learned to fear their attacks. The Nazis often called the female pilots the "Night Witches." Their skill and success in battle would make them heroes of the Soviet Union.

JOINING THE SQUADRONS

After the Nazi invasion, hundreds of Soviet women wrote to Marina Raskova. They wanted to serve their country as pilots, and they asked for her help.

Three years before the war, Raskova became famous for being part of a historic flight across the Soviet Union. Her crewmates broke the world record for the longest flight ever made by women.

Lieutenant Raskova, you parachuted from the airplane into the Siberian forest--in a snowstorm! Why did you do this dangerous thing?

We were almost out of fuel. After I jumped, the plane weighed less. My comrades were able to fly further and break the record.

Raskova was one of the most famous pilots in the country. She was greatly respected and knew the country's leader, Joseph Stalin.

It is too dangerous to have women fight as pilots.

People will not forgive us for sacrificing young girls.

These girls are already going to the front lines to fight, Comrade Stalin. They are taking matters into their own hands. Soon, they will even steal airplanes to protect the motherland.

We can't have girls fighting in a war. That's a job for men.

But comrade, these women are trained pilots. We need their help to defend the motherland.

In the end, Stalin agreed with Raskova's arguments. The Soviet military created three squadrons of women pilots. Raskova was named the commander.

Women came from across the Soviet Union to serve in the air squadrons. The military had no uniforms for women, so they had to wear men's uniforms.

Some of you have left school to be here. Some of you have left your own children behind. All of you have sworn to defend our motherland to the last breath!

Training was difficult. Most of the women had flown small planes before. But now they had to learn to fly fighters and bombers.

The women had several accidents during training. Many of the newer Soviet planes had been destroyed by the Nazis. So the women's squadrons had to train with older, broken-down planes.

Many of the male officers were against women having their own squadrons. But others knew that women could fly as well as men.

I've received 112 little princesses. Just what am I supposed to do with them?

They're not princesses. They're pilots. And they're here to fight, just like the men.

Women did the same jobs that the men did in their squadrons. Each one did her part.

Pilots flew the fighters and bombers into combat.

Navigators studied maps and plotted the course for the planes.

Armorers loaded the planes with bombs and ammunition for battle.

Mechanics made sure the planes worked properly.

BATTLES IN THE SKY

In 1942 the Nazis were at the height of their power. Their empire stretched across Europe.

Europe 1942

The Nazis believed that people in the Soviet Union were worth less than Germans. They ruled over the lands they conquered with terrible cruelty.

Axis-Controlled Territory

Allied Nations

Neutral Nations

Three Soviet women's squadrons were sent to fight on the front lines. They flew three types of planes on different missions.

DADADADADADA

Fighter planes fought to stop the Nazi air force from striking Soviet troops.

Dive bombers were used to keep German troops away from towns and cities.

ZIP! ZIP! PFFT! CHUK!

TRAT-TRAT-TRAT-TRATT

Slow-flying biplanes were often used for sneaky nighttime attacks. They bombed camps of German soldiers and supplies.

ZZZHEEEE ...

KA-BOOM!

The women who flew fighter planes tried to keep German bombers from attacking Soviet cities.

BRZBRZBRZBRZBRZ!

BRZBRZBRZBRZBRZ!

In April 1943, two female fighter pilots encountered a large force of enemy planes.

Commander, I count 42 enemy bombers approaching. I repeat, 42 bombers. What are our orders?

What are your orders? Attack! ATTACK!

The two pilots attacked the German bombers alone.

DADADADADA!

DADADADADA!

They shot down four of the German planes.

KA-PLEW!

We're under attack! It must be a squadron of fighters! Release your bombs and return to base!

Although they were outnumbered, the two Soviet women chased the rest of the bombers away. They saved a railway station and thousands of soldiers from being attacked.

Command, they're turning back. I repeat, the enemy is turning back!

13

Dive bomber pilots attacked Nazi forces with deadly accuracy.

Target is below. I'm going into our dive.

The pilots steered the plane into a steep dive toward the target.

When the plane was close to the ground, the pilot would release the bombs.

Bombs away!

vvzZVVZZVVZZVVZZVVZZVV

KA-BOOM!

KA-BOOM!

KA-BOOM!

The Soviet dive bomber attacks were deadly for Germany's forces. Nazi fighter pilots tried to shoot the Soviet planes out of the sky to protect the ground troops.

KA-POW! KA-POW! KA-POW!

TAT! TAT! TAT! TAT! TAT!

During one mission, the plane flown by Lyuba Gubina was hit by fighters.

We're hit!

TZING!

TZING!

We're going down! We have to bail out!

You go first! We'll find each other on the ground!

I can't get out! My parachute is caught!

Lyuba fought to keep the plane in the air, while the navigator worked to free herself.

I can't hold on much longer! Get out NOW!

The navigator managed to escape the plane. But Lyuba didn't have time to jump out. She gave her life to save her navigator's.

BOOM!

Lyuba! NO!

THE NIGHT WITCHES

The most famous of the Soviet women's squadrons was the 46th Night Bomber Regiment.

BRZBRZBRZBRZBRZ!

BRZBRZBRZBRZBRZ!

BRZBRZBRZBRZBRZ!

Target is ahead.
Attack formation.

They flew under the cover of night to attack German forces behind the front lines.

Hurry! We must have these shells ready for the attack.

As they approached their target, the night bomber pilots would turn off their biplanes' engines.

BRZBRZBRZBRZBRZ ... CLICK

The Night Witches' base was near the front lines. There were no lights for the runway, so that the Germans could not locate them.

Mechanics and armorers worked quickly in the darkness.

I have to replace these engine plugs.

Do it fast! We only have five minutes.

Fasten the bombs securely.

You'll first attack this supply base to the west. After you return, you'll have three more missions tonight.

There! It's the Night Witches!

KA-POW!

KA-POW!

KA-POW!

The Night Witches flew the Po-2 bomber. It was an old biplane that Soviet pilots had flown for many years. Because the planes were slow, they were easy targets for soldiers on the ground.

Antiaircraft fire was a terrible danger to the Night Witches. The bullets easily ripped through the old planes' canvas coverings.

We're hit!

ZIP!

I have to turn back. Our only chance is to land the plane somewhere.

ZIP!

The planes had to carry as many bombs as possible, so heavy parachute packs were left behind. If a plane was hit by enemy fire, the pilot and navigator could not bail out. Several brave Night Witches went down along with their planes.

SCREEEEE...

SCREEEEE...

SCREEEEE...

We're not going to make it! Prepare to crash!

21

DANGEROUS MISSIONS

That was our tenth mission tonight. And we have two more before sunrise.

The women who flew the night bombers faced many dangers. They dropped bombs on their targets, returned to the base for refueling, and then took off on the next mission.

I'm too tired to get out of the cockpit.

Here's some hot tea. It'll help you stay awake--and keep warm.

Many pilots and navigators were lost when their planes were shot down. One who survived was Nina Raspopova.

Nina and her navigator were flying in the mountains in southern Russia, in December 1942, when antiaircraft fire hit their plane.

BOOM!

ZIP!

We're hit! The whole bottom of the cockpit has been blown away.

We have to make a crash landing.

Nina managed to land the crippled plane. The navigator was badly wounded, but Nina freed her from the wreckage.

Nina was also injured. Antiaircraft fire had blasted the wooden frame of the airplane. She had large splinters stuck in her body.

Nina, it's too far back to our side of the lines. Go on without me. I'm too badly hurt.

No, I won't leave you. The Nazis will kill you. We can make it together.

The two women had a difficult trek back to their camp, but they made it safely. It took two months for Nina to recover from her injuries. But once healed, she went straight back to flying with the squadron.

23

During one mission Yevgenia Zhigulenko attacked a storage area of German weapons. Just after dropping the bombs, her plane was hit by antiaircraft fire.

ZIP!

ZIP!

ZIP!

ZIP!

BOOM!

BOOM!

The engine is stalling! We're rolling over! Hang on!

CHUG CHUG... CHUG CHUG... CHU-

Come on, engine! Start! Start!

CHU-... CHU-... CHUG... CHUGCHUG...

BRZBRZBRZBRZBRZ!

We're not going to make it back to base. Give me directions to someplace safe to land.

BRZBRZBRZBR... CHUGCHUG... BRZBRZBRZBRZBR... CHUG

Did you hear--?

NO!

Yevgenia managed to land the damaged plane on a beach.

HELP ... HELP

She must have fallen out when we rolled upside-down. How will we ever find her?

When the engine stalled, the navigator's seat broke off and fell to the bottom of the plane.

You're alive! But . . . how?

You won't believe this. My feet are stuck through the bottom of the plane. Help me get out.

25

VICTORY

Despite the Soviets' best efforts, the Germans kept winning battle after battle. They advanced deep into Soviet territory.

They're burning all of our crops. Our beautiful country is burning.

They're moving so fast. How can we stop them?

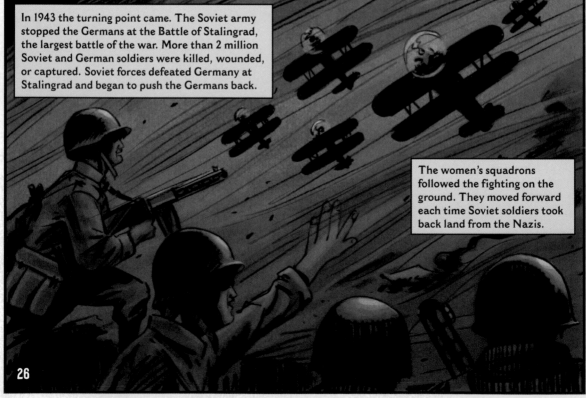

In 1943 the turning point came. The Soviet army stopped the Germans at the Battle of Stalingrad, the largest battle of the war. More than 2 million Soviet and German soldiers were killed, wounded, or captured. Soviet forces defeated Germany at Stalingrad and began to push the Germans back.

The women's squadrons followed the fighting on the ground. They moved forward each time Soviet soldiers took back land from the Nazis.

As the Soviet troops advanced, the women's missions became more difficult.

Soviet and German troops were soon fighting so close together that the pilots could not tell one side from the other.

One morning, the Night Witches were sleeping in their tents after flying all night. They heard soldiers outside. But they didn't know if the men were Soviet or German troops. They prepared to fight.

CLUNK

CLUNK

CLATTER

Shhhh. Don't let them know we're here.

Just in time, they realized the soldiers were on their side.

We've been fighting all night to push the Germans back. You won't have to worry about their antiaircraft guns anymore.

That's good news! Perhaps this hateful war will be over soon. Then we can go home.

HEROES OF THE MOTHERLAND

June 24, 1945. It was over. Nazi Germany was defeated. More than 40,000 Soviet soldiers marched through Moscow's Red Square in a great parade to celebrate the end of the war.

Members of the 46th Night Bomber Regiment took part in the parade. Many wore the Hero of the Soviet Union medal, the highest honor anyone in the Soviet military could receive.

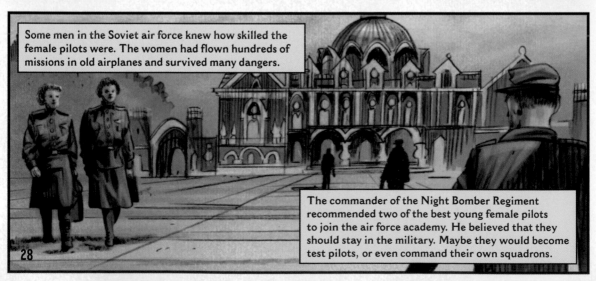

Some men in the Soviet air force knew how skilled the female pilots were. The women had flown hundreds of missions in old airplanes and survived many dangers.

The commander of the Night Bomber Regiment recommended two of the best young female pilots to join the air force academy. He believed that they should stay in the military. Maybe they would become test pilots, or even command their own squadrons.

But when the women arrived, the general of the academy called them to his office.

You are heroes of our Motherland. You showed what women can do when their help is needed.

But studying in the academy is hard work. You lost so much strength during the war, we must protect your health.

The pilots understood that the general was rejecting them.

Other women who served in the squadrons wanted to be finished with war. They hoped to return to their families and help rebuild their country.

Years later, pilot Nadia Popova said, *"Peace was the only thing we cared about. We just wanted to return to a normal life."*

Nadia had flown more than 850 missions during the war. Like all of the women she served with, Nadia was proud of the part she played in freeing her homeland.

Nadia earned several awards for her service, including Hero of the Soviet Union, the Order of Lenin, and the Order of the Red Banner. After the war, she worked as a flight instructor.

Later in life, Nadia remembered her time as one of the Night Witches. *"I can still imagine myself as a young girl, up there in my little bomber. And I ask myself, 'Nadia, how did you do it?'"*

29

GLOSSARY

academy (uh-KAD-uh-mee)—a school that teaches special subjects, such as skills needed to become an officer in the military

bail out (BAYL OUT)—to jump out of an airplane and parachute to safety

canvas (KAN-vuhs)—a type of strong, heavy cloth usually used to make tents and ship sails

cockpit (KOK-pit)—the area in an airplane where the pilot and navigator sit

comrade (KOM-rad)—a good friend, or someone you fight with in battle; people in the Soviet Union often called each other "comrade" to show that they were all working together for their country

front line (FRUHNT LYN)—the area nearest an enemy's position during a war

Nazi Germany (NOT-see JER-muh-nee)—a period of time from 1933 to 1945 when Germany was controlled by the Nazi Party and led by Adolph Hitler

Soviet Union (SOH-vee-et YOON-yuhn)—a former group of 15 republics that included Russia, Ukraine, and other nations of eastern Europe and northern Asia

squadron (SKWAHD-ruhn)—a military unit, often a group of military pilots and aircraft

stall (STAHL)—when a vehicle's engine suddenly stops running

READ MORE

Dell, Pamela. *The Soviet Night Witches: Brave Women Bomber Pilots of World War II*. Women and War. North Mankato, MN: Capstone Press, 2018.

Owens, Lisa L. *Women Pilots of World War II*. Heroes of World War II. Minneapolis: Lerner Publications, 2018.

Simons, Lisa M Bolt. *The U.S. WASP: Trailblazing Women Pilots of World War II*. Women and War. North Mankato, MN: Capstone Press, 2018.

CRITICAL THINKING QUESTIONS

- Some of the pilots who flew in the women's squadrons were only 17 years old. Imagine that you were one of these young women. Why would you leave your family and school to join an air force squadron and face terrible dangers?

- More than 26 million people in the Soviet Union died during World War II. Imagine if that many Americans had died in the war. What effect do you think that would have had on U.S. citizens? How would people in the United States remember the war today?

- The Night Witches showed great bravery during the war. But some male officers still opposed having women pilots in the air force. Why do you think they felt this way?

INTERNET SITES

Fearless Female Russion Pilots
https://www.dailymail.co.uk/news/article-4706856/Female-Soviet-pilots-transformed-colourised-WWII-photos.html

Meet the Night Witches
https://www.history.com/news/meet-the-night-witches-the-daring-female-pilots-who-bombed-nazis-by-night

The Night Witches
http://elinorflorence.com/blog/night-witches

INDEX